Teach Yourself Coding

A Beginner's Guide to Learn Programming in 30 Days

By A. J. Smales

Axon Press Self-Help Series © 2024   All Rights Reserved

Introduction:
Welcome to Your Coding Journey

Have you ever wondered how apps, websites, or even video games are created? Or perhaps you've heard people talk about coding and thought, *"That sounds amazing, but where would I even begin?"* The truth is, learning to code has never been easier—or more important—than it is today.

Coding is not just for computer scientists or tech geniuses. It's for **everyone**—students, professionals, creative minds, and problem-solvers. Whether you want to change careers, develop your own app, or simply explore a new skill, coding can open doors you never imagined. And the best part? You don't need a degree, expensive tools, or years of experience to start. You just need curiosity, a computer, and a willingness to learn.

This book is your step-by-step guide to **learning programming in 30 days**. It's designed specifically for beginners—people like you who may not have any experience but want to understand the basics, build simple projects, and gain the confidence to keep learning. You'll start with the fundamentals—what coding is, how it works, and why it matters—and progress through small, hands-on projects that will help you write real programs by the end of the month.

Why Learn to Code?

Coding is like a superpower in today's digital world. Here's what it can do for you:

- **Unlock Career Opportunities**: Many jobs in fields like tech, finance, healthcare, and design require basic coding skills. Learning to code makes you more employable and valuable in the workforce.
- **Boost Problem-Solving Skills**: Coding teaches you how to think logically and break big problems into small, manageable steps—skills that apply to every area of life.
- **Spark Creativity**: From building a website to automating daily tasks, coding allows you to create projects that bring your ideas to life.
- **Prepare for the Future**: The demand for programmers and tech skills is growing fast. Learning to code ensures you stay ahead in a changing world.

Coding isn't just a skill—it's a mindset. Once you learn it, you'll see the world differently. You'll start to notice the technology around you and understand how it works.

What You'll Learn

This book breaks coding into simple, practical lessons you can complete over 30 days. Here's what you'll gain:

- **Hands-On Coding Practice**: Each chapter includes easy-to-follow explanations, real-life examples, and beginner-friendly coding exercises.
- **Key Programming Concepts**: You'll learn about variables, loops, functions, and more—the building blocks of every programming language.
- **Confidence to Code**: By the end of this book, you'll have written multiple small programs and developed a strong foundation to explore more advanced coding projects.

We'll primarily use **Python**—one of the easiest and most popular programming languages for beginners. It's used by companies like Google, NASA, and Netflix and is perfect for learning the basics of coding.

How to Use This Book

- **One Step at a Time**: Each chapter builds on the previous one, so take your time and don't rush.
- **Write the Code Yourself**: The best way to learn is by doing. Try out the examples and exercises—don't worry if you make mistakes. Mistakes are part of learning!
- **Be Consistent**: Dedicate a little time each day to coding, even if it's just 30 minutes. Small, regular progress adds up to big results.

Let's Begin Your Journey

You don't need to know everything to start—you just need to start. This book will guide you every step of the way. By the end of 30 days, you'll have a strong foundation in programming, confidence in your skills, and the excitement to keep learning.

So, open your computer, take a deep breath, and get ready to write your first line of code.

Welcome to your coding journey—let's begin!

Table of Contents

1. Why Learn to Code? The Power of Programming
2. Getting Started: Setting Up Your Coding Environment
3. First Steps in Coding: Writing Your First Program
4. Programming Basics: Variables, Data Types, and Operations
5. Making Decisions: Conditional Statements
6. Loops: Repeating Tasks with Ease
7. Functions: Organizing and Reusing Code
8. Working with Lists and Loops
9. Understanding Errors: Debugging and Troubleshooting
10. Introduction to Objects and Basic OOP Concepts
11. Working with User Input and Simple Projects
12. Introduction to Web Development Basics
13. Small Coding Projects to Build Your Confidence
14. Next Steps: Exploring Coding Languages and Tools
15. Becoming a Lifelong Coder: Resources and Communities

Conclusion

- Your Journey to Coding Success

Chapter 1: Why Learn to Code? The Power of Programming

Coding is more than just typing lines of text into a computer—it's a gateway to solving problems, unlocking creativity, and shaping the future. In today's digital world, coding has become one of the most valuable and versatile skills you can learn, no matter your age, career, or background.

Coding: The Skill of the Future

The world is changing fast, and technology is at the center of it all. From smartphones and streaming platforms to self-driving cars and artificial intelligence, nearly everything you use in your daily life is powered by code. Learning to code means becoming a **creator** of technology, not just a user.

Why Coding Matters

1. **Career Opportunities**: Jobs that require coding skills are growing rapidly, and they aren't limited to the tech industry. Industries like finance, healthcare, education, and design all need people who can understand and use technology.
   - *Fact*: Coding jobs are among the highest-paying and fastest-growing careers worldwide.
2. **Problem-Solving Skills**: Coding teaches you how to break complex problems into smaller, manageable steps—a mindset that can help you in any career or life situation.
3. **Creativity and Innovation**: Coding allows you to build tools, apps, websites, and even games. It's a chance to turn your ideas into real projects.
4. **Future-Proof Your Skills**: As technology evolves, the demand for people who can code will only increase. Learning to code ensures you stay ahead in a rapidly changing world.

What Can You Do with Coding?

Coding isn't just about building software or working at big tech companies. Here are real-world examples of what you can do with coding:

- **Build Websites and Apps**: Create your own website, blog, or app to share your ideas with the world.
- **Automate Tasks**: Write simple programs to save time—like organizing files or scheduling reminders.
- **Analyze Data**: Learn how to process and visualize data to uncover insights (useful for business, science, and research).
- **Create Games and Tools**: Design your own games, puzzles, or interactive tools for fun or education.
- **Explore Robotics and AI**: Control robots, create smart devices, or work on artificial intelligence systems.

Real-Life Example: Many popular apps and websites today, like Facebook, Instagram, and YouTube, started as small coding projects created by individuals with an idea.

Success Stories: Self-Taught Coders Who Made It Big

Learning to code can be life-changing. Many people have taught themselves coding and gone on to achieve amazing things.

- **Chris Wanstrath**: Chris, a self-taught coder, co-founded GitHub, a platform now used by millions of developers worldwide.
- **Joy Buolamwini**: Joy used her coding skills to research bias in AI, leading global conversations about fairness in technology.
- **Mark Zuckerberg**: Mark famously started Facebook from his college dorm room with just an idea and coding skills.

Inspiration: These stories prove that you don't need to be a computer science expert to succeed—anyone can learn to code and create something meaningful.

Common Myths About Coding—Debunked

Many beginners hesitate to learn coding because of common misconceptions. Let's clear those up:

1. **Myth**: *"Coding is too hard for me."*
   - o **Truth**: Coding is like learning a new language. You start with simple words (concepts) and build up gradually. Anyone can learn it!
2. **Myth**: *"I'm not good at math, so I can't code."*
   - o **Truth**: While some coding uses math, you don't need to be a math genius to get started. Coding is more about logical thinking.
3. **Myth**: *"Coding takes years to learn."*
   - o **Truth**: You can learn the basics in a matter of weeks. With practice, you'll keep improving step by step.

What You'll Gain from Learning to Code

By learning to code, you'll gain:

- **Confidence**: The ability to solve problems and tackle challenges.
- **Creativity**: Tools to bring your ideas to life.
- **Flexibility**: Skills you can apply in any industry or career path.
- **Opportunity**: Access to jobs, projects, and innovations shaping the future.

Reflection: Why Do *You* Want to Learn to Code?

Before moving forward, take a moment to reflect:

1. What excites you about learning to code?
2. What problems would you like to solve, or what projects would you love to build?
3. What opportunities do you see for yourself as a programmer?

Write down your answers as a reminder of why you're starting this journey.

Your First Step Toward Coding Success

Learning to code may feel like a big challenge, but remember: **every great programmer started as a beginner.** By dedicating yourself to this book for the next 30 days, you'll gain the essential tools, skills, and confidence to write code and create your own projects.

In the next chapter, we'll set up everything you need to get started—your tools, environment, and mindset for success.

Let's begin this journey together. Your future as a coder starts now!

Chapter 2: Getting Started: Setting Up Your Coding Environment

Before you can begin writing code, you need a space to write and run it—this is called your **coding environment**. Just like an artist needs a canvas and tools or a chef needs a kitchen, programmers need the right software and setup to work efficiently.

This chapter will guide you step by step through setting up a simple, beginner-friendly coding environment, using tools like **VS Code** (Visual Studio Code) and **Replit**, so you're ready to write and run your very first program.

What Is a Coding Environment?

A coding environment is a combination of tools and software that allows you to write, test, and run your programs. It usually includes:

1. **A Text Editor or IDE (Integrated Development Environment)**: Where you write your code.
2. **A Compiler or Interpreter**: Software that translates your code into something the computer can understand.
3. **A Terminal**: Where you run your code to see the results.

Don't worry if these words sound new—by the end of this chapter, you'll understand how everything works together!

Choosing Your Coding Tools

For beginners, it's important to start with tools that are easy to use and widely supported. Here are two options we'll focus on:

1. **Visual Studio Code (VS Code)**
   - A free, lightweight, and powerful text editor. It works on Windows, macOS, and Linux.
   - VS Code is used by beginners and professionals alike.
2. **Replit**
   - A cloud-based tool that lets you write and run code right in your web browser.
   - No installation is needed—perfect if you want to start coding quickly.

Both options are excellent for getting started. You can choose the one that works best for you!

Option 1: Setting Up Visual Studio Code (VS Code)

Follow these steps to install and set up VS Code:

Step 1: Download VS Code

1. Go to the official VS Code website: https://code.visualstudio.com/.
2. Download the version for your operating system (Windows, macOS, or Linux).

Step 2: Install VS Code

1. Open the downloaded file and follow the installation instructions.
2. Once installed, open VS Code—it should look like a blank workspace.

Step 3: Install the Python Extension

1. In VS Code, go to the **Extensions** tab (click the square icon on the left side).
2. Search for "Python" and click **Install** on the extension by Microsoft.

This extension helps VS Code understand and run Python code.

Step 4: Install Python

To write and run Python code, you'll need Python installed on your computer:

1. Go to the official Python website: https://www.python.org/downloads/.
2. Download and install the latest version. Make sure to check **"Add Python to PATH"** during installation.

Testing Your Setup

1. In VS Code, create a new file called `hello.py`.
2. Type the following code:

```python
print("Hello, World!")
```

3. Save the file, right-click anywhere in the code, and select **Run Python File in Terminal**.
4. If everything is set up correctly, you'll see:

```
Hello, World!
```

Congratulations! You've written and run your first Python program.

Option 2: Getting Started with Replit

Replit is a simple way to start coding without downloading or installing anything. Follow these steps:

Step 1: Sign Up for Replit

1. Go to the Replit website: https://replit.com/.
2. Click **Sign Up** to create a free account. You can use your email or sign up with Google.

Step 2: Create a New Python Project

1. On the dashboard, click **Create Repl**.
2. Select **Python** from the list of languages.
3. Name your project (e.g., "First Program") and click **Create Repl**.

Step 3: Write and Run Code

1. In the code editor, type:

```python
print("Hello, World!")
```

2. Click the green **Run** button at the top.
3. You'll see this output in the terminal:

```
Hello, World!
```

That's it! Replit is ready to go, and you've written your first program.

Understanding Your Tools

Now that your coding environment is set up, let's look at the tools you'll use:

- **Text Editor (VS Code or Replit)**: Where you type your code.
- **The Run Button or Terminal**: This executes your program and shows the results.
- **Code Files**: Your code is saved in files, usually with the extension `.py` for Python.

Tip: As a beginner, don't worry if you make mistakes. Errors are part of coding, and you'll learn how to fix them as you go.

Troubleshooting Common Issues

If something doesn't work, don't panic! Here are common solutions:

1. **Python Not Found**: If Python isn't installed, reinstall it and check "Add to PATH" during installation.
2. **Code Doesn't Run**: Double-check your syntax and file names. Remember, Python is case-sensitive!
3. **Replit Errors**: Refresh the page or restart the program.

Reflection: Your Coding Environment Is Ready

Take a moment to celebrate—you've successfully set up your tools and written your first program! This setup will serve as your workspace for the rest of the book.

What's Next?

In the next chapter, we'll dive deeper into writing code and understanding the structure of a program. You'll learn how to store information using variables and work with basic data types like numbers and text.

Your tools are ready. Your coding journey has begun. Let's write some code!

Chapter 3: First Steps in Coding: Writing Your First Program

Welcome to the exciting world of coding! In this chapter, you'll write your very first program using **Python**, one of the easiest and most beginner-friendly programming languages. Don't worry if you feel nervous—every coder starts with the basics. By the end of this chapter, you'll understand how code is written, what "syntax" means, and how to run programs step by step.

Let's take the first step toward becoming a programmer!

What Is a Program?

A **program** is a set of instructions that tells a computer what to do. Just like following a recipe to bake a cake, a program provides step-by-step instructions for the computer to follow.

For example, here's what happens when you write a program:

1. **You write the code** (the instructions).
2. **The computer reads the code** and understands what you want.
3. **The computer executes the instructions** and produces a result.

Simple, right? Now let's write your first program to see how this works!

Your First Python Program: "Hello, World!"

The very first program every programmer writes is called **"Hello, World!"** It's a simple program that tells the computer to display the words "Hello, World!" on the screen. It might seem basic, but it's the first step in learning how programming works.

Step 1: Open Your Coding Environment

- If you're using **VS Code**, open your editor and create a new file called `hello.py`.
- If you're using **Replit**, create a new Python project.

Step 2: Write the Code

Type the following line into your file:

```python
print("Hello, World!")
```

- `print()`: This is a **function** in Python that tells the computer to display something on the screen.
- `"Hello, World!"`: These are the words we want to display. Anything inside quotation marks is called a **string** (text data).

Step 3: Run the Code

- In **VS Code**: Right-click on the file and select **Run Python File in Terminal**.
- In **Replit**: Click the green **Run** button at the top.

Output:

```
Hello, World!
```

Congratulations! You just wrote and ran your first program! 🎉

Breaking Down the Program

Here's what you've done:

- `print()`: This tells Python to display something.
- **Quotation Marks (" ")**: These tell Python that the words inside are text (a string).
- **Syntax**: Programming languages follow specific **rules**, just like grammar in a spoken language. Python's syntax is simple and easy to follow.

Key Point: In programming, every line of code has a purpose. Writing clean and correct syntax is important because the computer reads your instructions literally.

Adding Comments to Code

Comments are notes you add to your code to explain what it does. The computer ignores comments when running the program—they're just for you and other people reading the code.

To add a comment in Python, use the # symbol:

```python
# This program prints Hello, World!
print("Hello, World!")
```

Why Use Comments?

- To explain what your code does.
- To remind yourself why you wrote a specific line.
- To help others understand your code.

Tip: Always write comments to make your code easier to understand!

What Happens When Code Runs?

When you run a program, the computer follows these steps:

1. **Reads the code**: It reads your file line by line.
2. **Understands the instructions**: It figures out what each line means.
3. **Executes the code**: It performs the actions you described, like printing text to the screen.

Practice Time: Your Turn to Code

Let's try a few exercises to practice what you've learned so far:

Exercise 1: Print Your Name

Write a program that displays your name.

Example Code:

```python
print("My name is Alex.")
```

Output:

```csharp
My name is Alex.
```

Exercise 2: Add a Comment

Modify the program to include a comment that explains what it does.

Example Code:

```python
# This program prints my name
print("My name is Alex.")
```

Exercise 3: Print Two Lines

Write a program that prints two lines of text.

Example Code:

```python
python

print("I am learning to code.")
print("It's fun!")
```

Output:

```kotlin
kotlin

I am learning to code.
It's fun!
```

Troubleshooting Common Errors

If something doesn't work, don't worry—every programmer makes mistakes! Here are common errors to watch out for:

1. **Missing Quotation Marks**:
   - o Incorrect: `print(Hello, World!)`
   - o Correct: `print("Hello, World!")`
2. **Capitalization**: Python is case-sensitive.
   - o Incorrect: `Print("Hello")`
   - o Correct: `print("Hello")`
3. **Missing Parentheses**:
   - o Incorrect: `print "Hello"`
   - o Correct: `print("Hello")`

Reflection: What Did You Learn?

Take a moment to reflect on your progress:

1. What happens when you use the `print()` function?
2. How do you write comments in Python?
3. What steps do you follow to run your code?

What's Next?

You've written your first program and learned the basics of Python's syntax. Great job! 🎉

In the next chapter, we'll build on this foundation by learning about **variables**, **data types**, and how to store and use information in your programs.

Keep practicing, and remember—every programmer started right where you are now. You're on your way! 🚀

Chapter 4: Programming Basics: Variables, Data Types, and Operations

Now that you've written your first program, it's time to explore the **building blocks of programming**. At the heart of every program are three key ideas:

1. **Variables**: A way to store information.
2. **Data Types**: The kind of information you can work with (like numbers and text).
3. **Operations**: Actions you can perform on that information (like adding numbers or combining words).

In this chapter, you'll learn how to use variables, understand different data types, and perform basic operations in Python. By the end, you'll be able to write programs that store and manipulate information with ease.

What Are Variables?

A **variable** is like a container that holds a piece of information. You can give it a name and store data in it, such as numbers, words, or even results of calculations.

How to Create a Variable in Python

In Python, you don't need to tell the computer what type of data you're storing—just give the variable a name and assign a value using the = symbol.

Example:

```python
python

name = "Alex"          # A variable that stores text (a string)
age = 25               # A variable that stores a number
height = 5.9           # A variable that stores a decimal number (float)

print(name)            # Outputs: Alex
print(age)             # Outputs: 25
print(height)          # Outputs: 5.9
```

- **name, age,** and **height** are variables.
- The = sign assigns a value to the variable.

Data Types: Different Kinds of Information

There are several **data types** in Python. Here are the most common ones:

1. **String (str)**: Text data, written inside quotation marks.
   - Example: `"Hello, World!"`, `"Python"`.
2. **Integer (int)**: Whole numbers.
   - Example: `10`, `-5`, `100`.
3. **Float (float)**: Decimal numbers.
   - Example: `3.14`, `-2.5`.
4. **Boolean (bool)**: True or false values.
   - Example: `True`, `False`.

Checking the Data Type

You can use the `type()` function to check a variable's data type:

python

```python
name = "Alex"
age = 25
is_student = True

print(type(name))        # Outputs: <class 'str'>
print(type(age))         # Outputs: <class 'int'>
print(type(is_student))  # Outputs: <class 'bool'>
```

Basic Operations in Python

You can perform operations on data, such as math calculations or combining strings. Let's explore:

1. Math Operations

Python can handle basic math:

Operator	Action	Example	Result
+	Addition	5 + 3	8
−	Subtraction	10 − 4	6
*	Multiplication	2 * 3	6
/	Division	8 / 2	4.0
**	Exponentiation	2 ** 3	8
%	Remainder	10 % 3	1

Example Code:

```python
python

a = 10
b = 3

sum_result = a + b
product = a * b
remainder = a % b

print("Sum:", sum_result)          # Outputs: Sum: 13
print("Product:", product)         # Outputs: Product: 30
print("Remainder:", remainder)     # Outputs: Remainder: 1
```

2. String Operations

You can also work with strings using the + operator (concatenation) or repeat strings with *.

Example Code:

```python
greeting = "Hello"
name = "Alex"

message = greeting + ", " + name + "!"  # Combining strings
print(message)                          # Outputs: Hello,
Alex!

repeat = "Ha" * 3
print(repeat)                           # Outputs: HaHaHa
```

Input: Getting Data from the User

To make programs interactive, you can use the `input()` function to get data from the user.

Example:

```python
python
```

```python
name = input("What is your name? ")   # Prompts the user for input
print("Hello, " + name + "!")
```

Output:

```csharp
csharp
```

```
What is your name? Alex
Hello, Alex!
```

Key Note: The `input()` function always returns a string, even if the user enters a number. You can convert it to a different type using `int()` or `float()`.

Example:

```python
python
```

```python
age = input("How old are you? ")      # User enters: 25
age = int(age)                        # Convert input to an integer

print("Next year, you will be", age + 1)
```

Practice Exercises

Exercise 1: Simple Math

Write a program that takes two numbers, adds them, and displays the result.

Example:

```python
num1 = 5
num2 = 7

total = num1 + num2
print("The total is:", total)
```

Exercise 2: Combine Strings

Write a program that takes the user's first name and last name and prints a full greeting.

Exercise 3: Interactive Math

Ask the user for two numbers, multiply them, and display the result.

Troubleshooting Common Errors

Here are some common beginner errors and solutions:

1. **Missing Quotes**: Forgetting to use quotes around strings.
   - Incorrect: `name = Hello`
   - Correct: `name = "Hello"`
2. **Mixing Data Types**: Combining strings and numbers without conversion.
   - Incorrect: `print("Age: " + 25)`
   - Correct: `print("Age: " + str(25))`
3. **Invalid Variable Names**: Variable names cannot start with numbers or use spaces.
   - Incorrect: `1name = "Alex"`
   - Correct: `name1 = "Alex"`

Reflection: What Did You Learn?

Take a moment to think about what you've learned:

1. What is a variable?
2. What are the common data types in Python?
3. How can you perform math and string operations?

What's Next?

In the next chapter, we'll learn how to **make decisions** in your code using **if-else statements**. You'll create programs that respond differently based on user input or conditions.

Keep practicing—every line of code brings you one step closer to becoming a programmer! 🚀

Chapter 5: Making Decisions: Conditional Statements

Programming is all about teaching computers to make decisions based on certain conditions. In this chapter, you'll learn how to use **conditional statements**—specifically, **if-else statements**—to control the flow of a program. By the end, you'll be able to write programs that behave differently based on user input or specific rules, making your code dynamic and interactive.

What Are Conditional Statements?

Conditional statements allow you to tell a computer:

- *"If something is true, do this. Otherwise, do something else."*

This ability to make decisions is what makes programs smart and responsive.

Here's a simple example in plain language:

- **If it's raining**, take an umbrella.
- **Otherwise**, enjoy the sunshine.

In Python, we use `if`, `else`, and sometimes `elif` (else if) to create these decision-making steps.

The Basic If-Else Statement

The `if` statement checks if a condition is **True**. If it is, the code inside the `if` block runs. If not, the code inside the `else` block runs.

Syntax:

```python
if condition:
    # Code to run if the condition is True
else:
    # Code to run if the condition is False
```

Example:

```python
age = 18

if age >= 18:
    print("You are an adult.")
else:
    print("You are a minor.")
```

Output:

```sql
You are an adult.
```

Conditions and Comparison Operators

Conditions are logical statements that evaluate to either **True** or **False**. To write conditions, you use **comparison operators**:

Operator	Meaning	Example	Result
==	Equal to	5 == 5	True
!=	Not equal to	5 != 3	True
>	Greater than	7 > 3	True
<	Less than	3 < 7	True
>=	Greater than or equal to	10 >= 10	True
<=	Less than or equal to	5 <= 10	True

Example:

```python
number = 10

if number > 0:
    print("The number is positive.")
else:
    print("The number is not positive.")
```

Output:

```csharp
The number is positive.
```

Using Elif (Else If) for Multiple Conditions

The `elif` keyword allows you to check multiple conditions. If the first `if` condition is False, the program checks the next `elif` condition.

Syntax:

python

```
if condition1:
    # Code if condition1 is True
elif condition2:
    # Code if condition2 is True
else:
    # Code if none of the conditions are True
```

Example:

python

```
score = 85

if score >= 90:
    print("Grade: A")
elif score >= 80:
    print("Grade: B")
elif score >= 70:
    print("Grade: C")
else:
    print("Grade: F")
```

Output:

makefile

```
Grade: B
```

Logical Operators: Combining Conditions

Sometimes, you need to check more than one condition at a time. For this, you use **logical operators**:

Operator	Meaning	Example	Result
and	Both conditions must be True	(5 > 3) and (10 > 8)	True
or	At least one condition is True	(5 > 10) or (10 > 8)	True
not	Reverses the condition	not (5 > 3)	False

Example:

```python
age = 20
has_ID = True

if age >= 18 and has_ID:
    print("You can enter the club.")
else:
    print("You cannot enter the club.")
```

Output:

```
You can enter the club.
```

User Input and Conditions

Let's make the program interactive by adding user input and conditions.

Example:

```python
number = int(input("Enter a number: "))

if number % 2 == 0:
    print("The number is even.")
else:
    print("The number is odd.")
```

Output (User enters 4):

```csharp
The number is even.
```

Practice Exercises

Exercise 1: Positive, Negative, or Zero

Write a program that asks the user for a number and tells them if the number is positive, negative, or zero.

Exercise 2: Grade Calculator

Ask the user for a test score and display their grade using this scale:

- 90 or higher: A
- 80–89: B
- 70–79: C
- Below 70: F

Exercise 3: Can You Vote?

Ask the user for their age. If they are 18 or older, print "You can vote!" Otherwise, print "You cannot vote yet."

Troubleshooting Common Errors

1. **IndentationError**: Python requires consistent indentation. Use **4 spaces** for each block of code.
   - Incorrect:

     ```python
     if True:
     print("Hello")
     ```

   - Correct:

     ```python
     if True:
         print("Hello")
     ```

2. **SyntaxError**: Missing colons (`:`) after `if`, `elif`, or `else`.
   - Incorrect: `if x > 5 print("Hi")`
   - Correct: `if x > 5: print("Hi")`
3. **TypeError**: Mixing strings and numbers in comparisons.
   - Incorrect: `if "10" > 5:`
   - Solution: Convert data using `int()` or `str()` as needed.

Reflection: What Did You Learn?

Take a moment to review:

1. What is an `if-else` statement, and how does it work?
2. How can you use `elif` to check multiple conditions?
3. How do logical operators like `and` and `or` help you write smarter programs?

What's Next?

In the next chapter, we'll learn about **loops**, which allow you to repeat tasks without writing the same code over and over. You'll discover how to combine loops with conditional statements to make powerful and dynamic programs.

You're doing great—keep practicing, and let's keep coding!

Chapter 6: Loops: Repeating Tasks with Ease

In programming, we often need to repeat tasks multiple times, like counting numbers, checking a list, or printing a pattern. Writing the same line of code over and over would be inefficient and time-consuming. That's where **loops** come in! Loops allow you to repeat a block of code **automatically**, saving time and effort.

In this chapter, you'll learn how to use **for-loops** and **while-loops**, the two most common types of loops in Python. By the end, you'll be able to write programs that count, perform calculations, and even play games—all with just a few lines of code!

What Is a Loop?

A **loop** is a way to tell the computer to repeat a set of instructions until a certain condition is met. For example:

- "Count from 1 to 10."
- "Keep asking the user for a password until they get it right."
- "Print a star pattern with 5 rows."

Loops help you automate repetitive tasks so you don't have to write the same code multiple times.

The For-Loop:
Repeating Tasks a Set Number of Times

A **for-loop** repeats a block of code a specific number of times.

Syntax:

```python
for variable in range(start, stop, step):
    # Code to repeat
```

- **range()**: Generates a sequence of numbers.
    - start: Where to begin (default is 0).
    - stop: Where to stop (not included).
    - step: How much to increase by each time (default is 1).

Example 1: Counting Numbers

Let's use a for-loop to count from 1 to 5:

```python
for i in range(1, 6):
    print(i)
```

Output:

```
1
2
3
4
5
```

Example 2: Repeating a Message

Use a for-loop to print a message multiple times:

python

```
for i in range(3):
    print("Hello, World!")
```

Output:

```
Hello, World!
Hello, World!
Hello, World!
```

Example 3: Printing a Pattern

You can combine loops and print statements to create patterns:

python

```
for i in range(1, 6):
    print("*" * i)
```

Output:

markdown

```
*
**
***
****
*****
```

The While-Loop:
Repeating Until a Condition Is Met

A **while-loop** repeats a block of code as long as a certain condition is
True.

Syntax:

```python
while condition:
    # Code to repeat
```

The loop continues until the condition becomes False.

Example 1: Counting with a While-Loop

python

```python
count = 1

while count <= 5:
    print(count)
    count += 1   # Increases count by 1
```

Output:

```
1
2
3
4
5
```

Explanation:

- The loop starts with count = 1.
- It checks the condition count <= 5.
- Inside the loop, the program prints the number and increases count by 1.

Example 2: Guessing Game

You can use a while-loop to keep asking the user for input until they guess correctly:

python

```python
secret_number = 7
guess = 0

while guess != secret_number:
    guess = int(input("Guess the number: "))
    if guess < secret_number:
        print("Too low! Try again.")
    elif guess > secret_number:
        print("Too high! Try again.")

print("Congratulations! You guessed it.")
```

Sample Output:

yaml

```
Guess the number: 5
Too low! Try again.
Guess the number: 10
Too high! Try again.
Guess the number: 7
Congratulations! You guessed it.
```

For-Loop vs While-Loop: When to Use Each

For-Loop	While-Loop
Use when you know **exactly how many times** to repeat the code.	Use when you need to repeat **until a condition changes**.
Example: Counting numbers, printing patterns.	Example: Waiting for user input, validating conditions.

Combining Loops and Conditions

You can combine loops with **if-else statements** to create more powerful programs.

Example: Finding Even Numbers

```python
for i in range(1, 11):
    if i % 2 == 0:  # Checks if the number is even
        print(i, "is even")
```

Output:

```csharp
2 is even
4 is even
6 is even
8 is even
10 is even
```

Practice Exercises

1. **Count Down**: Write a program that uses a while-loop to count down from 10 to 1 and then prints "Blast off!".
2. **Multiplication Table**: Use a for-loop to print the multiplication table for a number (e.g., 2 times table).
3. **Password Checker**: Write a program that keeps asking the user for a password until they enter the correct one.
4. **Print a Pyramid**: Use a for-loop to print a pyramid pattern like this:

```markdown
    *
   * * *
  * * * * *
 * * * * * *
```

Troubleshooting Common Loop Errors

1. **Infinite Loop**: A loop that never ends because the condition is always `True`.
   - o **Fix**: Make sure the loop condition changes inside the loop.

   Example (Fixed):

   python

   ```python
   count = 1
   while count <= 5:
       print(count)
       count += 1  # This ensures the condition will
   become False
   ```

2. **Off-by-One Error**: Starting or ending a loop at the wrong number.
   - o **Tip**: Use `print()` statements to debug and check your ranges.
3. **IndentationError**: Forgetting to indent code inside a loop.
   - o Always indent the code block inside `for` and `while` loops.

Reflection: What Did You Learn?

Take a moment to review:

1. What is the difference between a **for-loop** and a **while-loop**?
2. How can you combine loops with **if-else statements**?
3. What are some practical uses for loops in programming?

What's Next?

In the next chapter, we'll learn how to make your programs even more organized and powerful by using **functions**. Functions allow you to write reusable blocks of code to simplify your programs.

Keep practicing—loops are a game-changer in programming!

Chapter 7: Functions: Organizing and Reusing Code

As your programs grow, writing the same code over and over can quickly become messy and hard to manage. **Functions** solve this problem by allowing you to organize your code into small, reusable blocks. Think of functions as mini-programs that you can create once and use as many times as you need.

In this chapter, you'll learn:

1. What functions are and why they're useful.
2. How to create, use, and reuse functions.
3. How to work with **parameters** (inputs) and **return values** (outputs).

By the end, you'll be able to write cleaner, more organized programs that are easier to read and maintain.

What Is a Function?

A **function** is a block of code that performs a specific task. You define the function once, and then you can **call** (use) it whenever you need it.

Why Use Functions?

1. **Reusability**: Write code once and use it multiple times.
2. **Organization**: Break long programs into smaller, manageable pieces.
3. **Readability**: Functions make code easier to understand.
4. **Avoid Repetition**: Instead of copying the same code, you just call the function.

Analogy: Imagine a function as a coffee machine. You press a button (call the function), and the machine makes coffee (performs a task). You don't need to know how the machine works—you just use it!

Creating and Calling Functions

To use a function, you must **define** it first, and then **call** it to make it run.

Defining a Function

You define a function in Python using the `def` keyword:

python

```
def say_hello():              # Function name: say_hello
    print("Hello, World!")   # Code inside the function
```

- **def**: Starts the function definition.
- **say_hello**: The name of the function. You can choose any descriptive name.
- **()**: Parentheses go after the function name.

Calling a Function

To make the function run, just write its name followed by `()`:

python

```
say_hello()   # Call the function
```

Output:

```
Hello, World!
```

Using Parameters: Giving Inputs to Functions

Functions can accept **parameters**—information you pass into the function to customize its behavior.

Example: Function with Parameters

python

```
def greet(name):                    # name is a parameter
    print("Hello, " + name + "!")

greet("Alice")                      # Passing 'Alice' as an
argument
greet("Bob")                        # Passing 'Bob' as an
argument
```

Output:

```
Hello, Alice!
Hello, Bob!
```

- **name** is a parameter that acts like a placeholder inside the function.
- When calling the function, you provide a value (argument) for the parameter.

Multiple Parameters

You can pass multiple parameters into a function.

Example:

python

```python
def add_numbers(a, b):  # Two parameters: a and b
    total = a + b
    print("The total is:", total)

add_numbers(5, 3)
add_numbers(10, 7)
```

Output:

csharp

```
The total is: 8
The total is: 17
```

Returning Values: Getting Outputs from Functions

Sometimes, you want a function to **return** a result instead of just printing it. Use the `return` keyword to send a value back to the program.

Example: Function with Return Value

python

```
def square(number):
    return number * number   # Returns the square of the
number

result = square(4)              # Store the result in a
variable
print("The square is:", result)
```

Output:

csharp

```
The square is: 16
```

- The `return` keyword sends the result back to the program.
- You can use the returned value later in your code (like storing it in a variable).

Combining Functions with Loops and Conditions

Functions can be used with loops and if-else statements to build more powerful programs.

Example: Check Even or Odd

```python
python

def check_even_odd(number):
    if number % 2 == 0:
        return "even"
    else:
        return "odd"

for i in range(1, 6):   # Loop through numbers 1 to 5
    result = check_even_odd(i)
    print(f"{i} is {result}")
```

Output:

```csharp
csharp

1 is odd
2 is even
3 is odd
4 is even
5 is odd
```

Practice Exercises

1. **Greeting Function**: Write a function `greet_user(name)` that takes a name as input and prints "Hello, [name]!".
2. **Addition Function**: Write a function `add(a, b)` that takes two numbers as inputs and returns their sum. Call the function with different numbers and print the results.
3. **Square Function**: Write a function `square(n)` that returns the square of a number. Print the square of numbers from 1 to 5 using a loop.
4. **Temperature Converter**: Write a function `celsius_to_fahrenheit(celsius)` that converts a Celsius temperature to Fahrenheit using the formula:

$$\text{Fahrenheit} = \text{Celsius} \times \frac{9}{5} + 32$$

Test the function with different temperatures.

Troubleshooting Common Function Errors

1. **IndentationError**: Make sure the code inside the function is indented properly.
   - o Correct:

   ```python
   def say_hello():
       print("Hello!")
   ```

2. **Missing Parentheses**: Don't forget `()` when calling a function.
   - o Incorrect: `say_hello`
   - o Correct: `say_hello()`
3. **Missing Arguments**: If a function requires parameters, you must provide them.
   - o Incorrect: `greet()`
   - o Correct: `greet("Alice")`

Reflection: What Did You Learn?

Take a moment to think about:

1. What are the benefits of using functions in a program?
2. How do parameters and return values make functions more flexible?
3. How can you reuse functions to simplify your code?

What's Next?

In the next chapter, we'll explore how to use **lists** to store and manage multiple pieces of data. You'll learn how to combine lists and loops to process data efficiently.

You're making great progress—keep practicing, and let's move to the next level!

Chapter 8: Working with Lists and Loops

In programming, we often need to work with multiple pieces of data, like a list of names, scores, or tasks. Instead of creating separate variables for each piece of data, we use **lists**—one of the most powerful tools in Python.

In this chapter, you'll learn how to:

1. Create, access, and modify lists.
2. Use loops to work with list data efficiently.
3. Build practical projects like to-do lists, score trackers, and simple data processors.

By combining lists with loops, you'll be able to manage large amounts of data with just a few lines of code!

What Is a List?

A **list** is a collection of items stored together in a single variable. Lists can hold:

- **Numbers**: [1, 2, 3]
- **Text**: ["Alice", "Bob", "Charlie"]
- **Mixed Data**: [1, "Hello", 3.14]

Lists are defined using square brackets [ ], with items separated by commas.

Example: Creating a List

python

```python
fruits = ["apple", "banana", "cherry"]  # A list of strings
numbers = [10, 20, 30, 40]              # A list of numbers
mixed = ["Hello", 42, 3.14]             # A list with mixed
data types

print(fruits)                           # Outputs: ['apple',
'banana', 'cherry']
```

Accessing Items in a List

Each item in a list has a position, called an **index**. In Python, the first item starts at index **0**.

Example: Access List Items

python

```python
fruits = ["apple", "banana", "cherry"]

print(fruits[0])    # Outputs: apple (first item)
print(fruits[1])    # Outputs: banana (second item)
print(fruits[-1])   # Outputs: cherry (last item)
```

Modifying Items in a List

You can change the value of a specific item by accessing its index.

Example:

```python
fruits = ["apple", "banana", "cherry"]

fruits[1] = "blueberry"  # Change 'banana' to 'blueberry'

print(fruits)            # Outputs: ['apple', 'blueberry',
'cherry']
```

Adding and Removing Items

Python provides methods to add and remove items in a list:

Action	Method	Example
Add an item to the end	append()	fruits.append("orange")
Insert at a position	insert(index, item)	fruits.insert(1, "kiwi")
Remove an item	remove(item)	fruits.remove("apple")
Remove last item	pop()	fruits.pop()

Example:

```python
fruits = ["apple", "banana", "cherry"]

fruits.append("orange")   # Add 'orange'
fruits.remove("banana")   # Remove 'banana'
fruits.insert(1, "kiwi")  # Insert 'kiwi' at index 1

print(fruits)             # Outputs: ['apple', 'kiwi',
'cherry', 'orange']
```

Using Loops with Lists

Loops make it easy to work with all items in a list.

Example: Loop Through a List

python

```python
fruits = ["apple", "banana", "cherry"]

for fruit in fruits:        # Loop through the list
    print(fruit)
```

Output:

```
apple
banana
cherry
```

Example: Finding the Total of a List

You can use a for-loop to calculate the total of all numbers in a list.

python

```python
numbers = [10, 20, 30, 40]
total = 0

for num in numbers:
    total += num  # Add each number to the total

print("Total:", total)
```

Output:

```makefile
Total: 100
```

Combining Lists and Conditions

You can use loops with `if` statements to filter or process data in a list.

Example: Finding Even Numbers

```python
numbers = [1, 2, 3, 4, 5, 6]

for num in numbers:
    if num % 2 == 0:   # Check if the number is even
        print(num, "is even")
```

Output:

```csharp
2 is even
4 is even
6 is even
```

Practical Projects

Project 1: To-Do List

Create a simple to-do list program where the user can add tasks:

python

```python
tasks = []   # Empty list to store tasks

print("To-Do List: Type 'done' to stop.")

while True:
    task = input("Add a task: ")
    if task.lower() == "done":
        break
    tasks.append(task)

print("Your To-Do List:")
for t in tasks:
    print("- " + t)
```

Project 2: Score Tracker

Write a program that calculates the average score of a list of grades:

python

```python
scores = [85, 90, 78, 92, 88]
total = sum(scores)   # Calculate total using sum()
average = total / len(scores)

print("Scores:", scores)
print("Average Score:", average)
```

Project 3: Filter Positive Numbers

Write a program that filters only positive numbers from a list:

python

```
numbers = [-5, 3, -1, 7, 0, -2, 8]
positives = []

for num in numbers:
    if num > 0:
        positives.append(num)

print("Positive Numbers:", positives)
```

Troubleshooting Common Errors

1. **IndexError**: Trying to access an index that doesn't exist.
   - Fix: Ensure the index is within the list length.
2. **TypeError**: Using the wrong data type.
   - Example: Adding a string to a list of numbers without conversion.
3. **Infinite Loops**: When using `while` loops, ensure the condition eventually becomes `False`.

Reflection: What Did You Learn?

Take a moment to review:

1. What is a list, and how do you create one?
2. How do you add, modify, and remove items from a list?
3. How can loops help you work with list data efficiently?

What's Next?

In the next chapter, we'll learn about **understanding errors** and the art of debugging—an essential skill for every programmer. You'll discover how to read error messages, find mistakes, and fix them with confidence.

You're doing amazing—keep practicing, and let's keep coding!

Chapter 9: Understanding Errors: Debugging and Troubleshooting

Every programmer—no matter how experienced—encounters errors. In fact, errors are a natural and important part of coding. They help you learn, improve, and make your programs stronger. The key is to understand what these errors mean and know how to fix them.

In this chapter, you'll learn:

1. The most common types of errors in Python.
2. How to read error messages.
3. Debugging techniques to find and fix problems in your code.

By the end of this chapter, you'll have the tools and confidence to troubleshoot your code like a pro!

What Are Errors in Programming?

An **error** happens when something in your code doesn't follow the rules of the programming language or behaves in an unexpected way. Python will stop running the program and display an **error message** to tell you what went wrong.

There are three main types of errors:

1. **Syntax Errors**: Problems with the rules of the language.
2. **Runtime Errors**: Errors that happen while the program is running.
3. **Logic Errors**: The program runs but produces the wrong result.

---

1. Syntax Errors: Breaking the Rules

A **syntax error** happens when Python doesn't understand what you've typed. It's like a grammar mistake in a sentence.

Common Causes:

- Missing colons : in `if`, `else`, `for`, or `def`.
- Missing or unmatched parentheses, brackets, or quotes.
- Incorrect indentation.

Example:

```python
if True
    print("Hello")
```

Error Message:

```javascript
SyntaxError: expected ':'
```

Fix: Add the missing colon.

```python
if True:
    print("Hello")
```

2. Runtime Errors: Crashing While Running

A **runtime error** occurs when your program starts running but crashes because of an issue that Python can't solve.

Common Causes:

- Dividing by zero.
- Using the wrong data type (e.g., adding a string to a number).
- Accessing an index that doesn't exist in a list.

Example: Division by Zero

```python
number = 10
result = number / 0
```

Error Message:

```vbnet
ZeroDivisionError: division by zero
```

Fix: Check for zero before performing the division.

```python
if number != 0:
    result = number / number
else:
    print("Cannot divide by zero.")
```

3. Logic Errors: The Silent Mistakes

A **logic error** is tricky because the program runs without any error message, but the output is incorrect. This happens when your code doesn't do what you intended.

Example:

You want to add two numbers, but you accidentally multiply them:

python

```
a = 5
b = 3
result = a * b   # Incorrect logic
print("Sum:", result)
```

Output:

makefile

```
Sum: 15
```

Fix: Check the logic and use the correct operator:

python

```
result = a + b   # Fix: Use addition instead of
multiplication
print("Sum:", result)
```

How to Read an Error Message

When Python finds an error, it stops the program and gives you an **error message**. Here's what an error message looks like:

```python
numbers = [1, 2, 3]
print(numbers[5])
```

Error Message:

```sql
IndexError: list index out of range
```

How to Read It:

1. **Error Type**: `IndexError` tells you what kind of error occurred.
2. **Description**: `list index out of range` explains what went wrong.
3. **Line Number**: Python highlights the exact line where the error occurred.

Use this information to find the mistake and fix it!

Debugging: Fixing Problems in Your Code

Debugging means finding and fixing errors in your code. Here are some tips to make debugging easier:

1. **Read the Error Message**: Start by understanding what Python is telling you.
2. **Print Statements**: Use `print()` to check the value of variables at different points in your code.

   Example:

   ```python
   x = 10
   y = 0
   print("x =", x, "y =", y)   # Debugging step
   result = x / y
   ```

3. **Break the Code into Steps**: Test small parts of your program one at a time to find where the problem is.
4. **Check Data Types**: Use the `type()` function to ensure variables are the correct type.
5. **Take a Break**: Sometimes stepping away from your code helps you see the problem with fresh eyes.

Practice Debugging

Exercise 1: Fix the Syntax Error

The following code has a syntax error. Fix it:

python

```
for i in range(5)
    print(i)
```

Exercise 2: Fix the Runtime Error

What's wrong with this program?

python

```
numbers = [10, 20, 30]
print(numbers[3])
```

Exercise 3: Fix the Logic Error

This code is supposed to calculate the square of a number but gives the wrong result:

python

```
number = 4
square = number * 2
print("Square:", square)
```

Reflection: What Did You Learn?

Take a moment to think about:

1. What are the three main types of errors in programming?
2. How do you read an error message to find and fix problems?
3. What debugging techniques can help you troubleshoot your code?

What's Next?

In the next chapter, we'll explore how to **work with files** to read and save data, allowing you to create more advanced and useful programs.

Remember: Every error is an opportunity to learn. Keep coding and debugging—you're getting better with every mistake!

Chapter 10: Introduction to Objects and Basic OOP Concepts

As programs grow larger and more complex, organizing your code becomes essential. **Object-Oriented Programming (OOP)** is a powerful way to structure programs by grouping related data and functions into reusable blocks called **objects**. OOP makes it easier to write clean, organized, and maintainable code.

In this chapter, you'll learn:

1. What Object-Oriented Programming is and why it's useful.
2. Basic OOP concepts: **classes**, **objects**, **attributes**, and **methods**.
3. How to create and use objects with simple, real-world examples.

By the end, you'll understand the foundation of OOP and be ready to use it in your own programs.

What Is Object-Oriented Programming?

Object-Oriented Programming (OOP) is a way of organizing your code around **objects**, which represent real-world things or concepts. An object can have:

1. **Attributes**: Characteristics or data about the object.
2. **Methods**: Actions or behaviors that the object can perform.

Analogy: Objects in the Real World

Imagine a **car** as an object:

- **Attributes** (data): color, brand, speed, fuel level.
- **Methods** (actions): start, stop, accelerate, brake.

Using OOP, we can represent a car in code as an **object** with attributes and methods, making our programs more intuitive and modular.

Classes and Objects: The Basics

A **class** is like a blueprint for creating objects. It defines what attributes and methods an object will have.

An **object** is an actual instance of a class—like a house built from a blueprint.

Defining a Class

You define a class in Python using the `class` keyword:

python

```
class Car:   # Class name: Car
    def __init__(self, brand, color):   # The constructor
        self.brand = brand              # Attribute: brand
        self.color = color              # Attribute: color
```

- **`__init__()`**: This is a special method (called a **constructor**) that runs when you create an object. It sets up the object's attributes.
- **`self`**: Refers to the object being created. It allows you to access the object's attributes and methods.

Creating an Object (Instantiation)

Once you have a class, you can create objects from it. This is called **instantiation**.

python

```
# Create objects of the Car class
car1 = Car("Toyota", "Red")
car2 = Car("Ford", "Blue")

# Access attributes
print(car1.brand)   # Outputs: Toyota
print(car2.color)   # Outputs: Blue
```

- **car1 and car2** are objects (instances) of the Car class.
- You can access their attributes using dot notation: object.attribute.

Adding Methods to a Class

Methods are functions inside a class that define actions the object can perform.

Example: Add a method to start the car

python

```
class Car:
    def __init__(self, brand, color):
        self.brand = brand
        self.color = color

    def start(self):  # Method to start the car
        print(f"The {self.color} {self.brand} is
starting.")

# Create an object
my_car = Car("Honda", "Black")
my_car.start()   # Call the method
```

Output:

csharp

```
The Black Honda is starting.
```

Real-World Example: Modeling a Person

Let's model a **Person** using a class. A person can have attributes like a name and age and methods like greeting someone.

```python
class Person:
    def __init__(self, name, age):
        self.name = name
        self.age = age

    def greet(self):  # Method to greet
        print(f"Hello, my name is {self.name}, and I am
{self.age} years old.")

# Create objects
person1 = Person("Alice", 25)
person2 = Person("Bob", 30)

# Call the greet method
person1.greet()
person2.greet()
```

Output:

```csharp
Hello, my name is Alice, and I am 25 years old.
Hello, my name is Bob, and I am 30 years old.
```

Key Concepts of OOP

Here's a summary of the core OOP concepts introduced so far:

1. **Class**: A blueprint for creating objects.
2. **Object**: An instance of a class.
3. **Attributes**: Data that describes the object (e.g., name, color).
4. **Methods**: Functions that define what the object can do.
5. **Constructor (__init__)**: A special method that initializes an object's attributes when it's created.

Practice Exercises

1. **Create a Pet Class**
    o   Define a `Pet` class with attributes like `name` and `animal_type` (e.g., dog, cat).
    o   Add a method `speak()` that prints a sound based on the animal type.
2. **Create a Bank Account Class**
    o   Define a `BankAccount` class with attributes `account_holder` and `balance`.
    o   Add methods to `deposit()` and `withdraw()` money.
3. **Student Class**
    o   Create a `Student` class with attributes like `name` and `grade`.
    o   Add a method `show_grade()` to display the student's grade.

Troubleshooting Common OOP Errors

1. **TypeError: Missing Arguments**
   - Happens when you forget to provide all the required attributes when creating an object.
   - Fix: Ensure you pass all arguments in the constructor.
2. **AttributeError**
   - Happens when you try to access an attribute or method that doesn't exist.
   - Fix: Check for typos or define the missing attribute/method.
3. **IndentationError**
   - Happens when class methods or code blocks are not properly indented.

Reflection: What Did You Learn?

Take a moment to think about:

1. What is a class, and how do you create one?
2. How do attributes and methods help define an object?
3. How can you use OOP to represent real-world things in code?

What's Next?

In the next chapter, we'll explore **working with files**—learning how to read, write, and save data to external files. Combining OOP with file operations will open up even more possibilities for creating powerful programs!

Keep practicing—understanding OOP will help you write clean and professional code!

Chapter 11: Working with User Input and Simple Projects

A great program doesn't just run—it interacts with the user! By allowing users to enter data, you can make programs dynamic, responsive, and fun. Whether it's asking questions, performing calculations, or running a quiz, user input is key to building interactive applications.

In this chapter, you'll learn:

1. How to **accept and validate user input** in Python.
2. Techniques for handling different types of input (numbers, text).
3. How to combine input with previous concepts like loops, conditions, and functions.
4. Build simple, fun projects: **a basic calculator**, **a quiz app**, and a **text-based adventure game**.

By the end, you'll see how all your programming skills come together to create practical and enjoyable programs.

Accepting User Input

Python makes it easy to get input from the user with the `input()` function.

Basic User Input

```python
name = input("What is your name? ")
print("Hello, " + name + "!")
```

Output:

```csharp
What is your name? Alice
Hello, Alice!
```

- **`input()`**: Prompts the user for input.
- The result is always returned as a **string**. If you need a number, you must **convert** it.

Converting User Input

To work with numbers, use `int()` or `float()` to convert the input:

python

```
age = int(input("How old are you? "))
print("Next year, you will be", age + 1)
```

Output:

sql

```
How old are you? 25
Next year, you will be 26
```

- **int()**: Converts input to an integer.
- **float()**: Converts input to a decimal (floating-point) number.

Validating User Input

Sometimes users enter invalid input (e.g., letters instead of numbers). Use loops and conditions to handle errors.

Example: Asking for a Valid Number

python

```
while True:
    try:
        number = int(input("Enter a number: "))
        break   # Exit the loop if input is valid
    except ValueError:
        print("That's not a valid number. Try again!")

print("You entered:", number)
```

Explanation:

- **try** and **except** catch errors (like invalid input).
- The loop repeats until the user provides valid input.

Project 1: Basic Calculator

Let's build a simple calculator that performs addition, subtraction, multiplication, and division.

python

```python
def calculator():
    print("Simple Calculator")
    print("Options: add, subtract, multiply, divide")

    while True:
        operation = input("Choose an operation (or 'exit'
to quit): ").lower()

        if operation == "exit":
            print("Goodbye!")
            break

        if operation not in ["add", "subtract", "multiply",
"divide"]:
            print("Invalid operation. Try again.")
            continue

        try:
            num1 = float(input("Enter the first number: "))
            num2 = float(input("Enter the second number:
"))
        except ValueError:
            print("Invalid input. Please enter numbers
only.")
            continue

        if operation == "add":
            print("Result:", num1 + num2)
        elif operation == "subtract":
            print("Result:", num1 - num2)
        elif operation == "multiply":
            print("Result:", num1 * num2)
        elif operation == "divide":
            if num2 == 0:
                print("Cannot divide by zero!")
```

```
        else:
            print("Result:", num1 / num2)

calculator()
```

Features:

- Handles invalid input and division by zero.
- Allows the user to perform multiple operations until they exit.

Project 2: Quiz Application

Test the user with a fun, interactive quiz.

python

```python
def quiz():
    print("Welcome to the Quiz Game!")
    score = 0

    # Question 1
    answer = input("1. What is the capital of France? ").lower()
    if answer == "paris":
        print("Correct!")
        score += 1
    else:
        print("Wrong. The correct answer is Paris.")

    # Question 2
    answer = input("2. What is 5 + 3? ")
    if answer == "8":
        print("Correct!")
        score += 1
    else:
        print("Wrong. The correct answer is 8.")

    # Question 3
    answer = input("3. What color is the sky on a clear day? ").lower()
    if answer == "blue":
        print("Correct!")
        score += 1
    else:
        print("Wrong. The correct answer is blue.")

    print(f"Your final score is {score}/3. Well done!")

quiz()
```

Features:

- Tracks and displays the user's score.
- Handles case sensitivity with `.lower()`.

Project 3: Text-Based Adventure Game

A fun and simple game where users make choices to navigate through a story.

python

```python
def adventure_game():
    print("Welcome to the Adventure Game!")
    print("You are in a dark forest. Two paths lie ahead.")

    choice = input("Do you take the 'left' path or the
'right' path? ").lower()

    if choice == "left":
        print("You encounter a friendly wizard who gives
you gold. You win!")
    elif choice == "right":
        print("You fall into a pit. Game over!")
    else:
        print("Invalid choice. The forest swallows you
whole!")

adventure_game()
```

Features:

- Simple decision-making with user input.
- Demonstrates how to branch the program flow based on choices.

Key Takeaways

1. **Accept Input**: Use `input()` to get data from users. Convert it using `int()` or `float()` for numbers.
2. **Validate Input**: Use loops and `try-except` to handle invalid input gracefully.
3. **Combine Skills**: Use loops, conditions, and functions to build interactive projects.

Practice Exercises

1. **Guess the Number Game**: Create a program where the user guesses a number between 1 and 10. Tell them if their guess is too high, too low, or correct.
2. **Simple To-Do List**: Allow users to add tasks to a list, view tasks, and remove completed ones.
3. **Rock-Paper-Scissors**: Let the user play Rock-Paper-Scissors against the computer. Use random choices for the computer's move.

Reflection: What Did You Learn?

Take a moment to review:

1. How do you accept and validate user input?
2. How can user input make programs more interactive?
3. How did the simple projects bring together everything you've learned so far?

What's Next?

In the final chapter, we'll look at how to **save and share your programs**, including writing to files, sharing your code, and planning your next steps as a programmer.

You've come a long way—get ready to finish strong!

Chapter 12: Introduction to Web Development Basics

Coding isn't limited to creating software or games—it also powers the web. Every website you visit is built using code, and understanding web development opens up endless opportunities to showcase your work, build portfolios, and even create businesses.

In this chapter, you'll learn:

1. The basics of **HTML** (the structure of a webpage).
2. An introduction to **CSS** (making webpages look great).
3. How Python or similar programming languages can work with web technologies.
4. How to build a simple webpage to tie everything together.

By the end, you'll have created your first webpage and understand how code connects to the web.

How Websites Work

When you visit a website, your browser (like Chrome or Firefox) loads code that tells it:

- **What to display**: This is done with **HTML**.
- **How it looks**: This is controlled with **CSS**.
- **How it works (interactivity)**: Programming languages like **Python** or **JavaScript** add functionality.

In this chapter, we'll focus on **HTML** and **CSS**—the building blocks of every webpage—and briefly explore how Python can interact with the web.

HTML: The Structure of a Webpage

HTML stands for **HyperText Markup Language**. It defines the structure of a webpage using **tags**. Tags tell the browser how to organize content like headings, paragraphs, images, and links.

Basic HTML Structure

Here's an example of a simple HTML webpage:

html

```
<!DOCTYPE html>
<html>
  <head>
    <title>My First Webpage</title> <!-- Title in the
browser tab -->
  </head>
  <body>
    <h1>Welcome to My Webpage</h1> <!-- Main heading -->
    <p>Hello, world! This is my first webpage.</p> <!--
Paragraph -->
    <a href="https://www.google.com">Click here to visit
Google</a> <!-- Link -->
  </body>
</html>
```

Explanation:

- **`<!DOCTYPE html>`**: Tells the browser this is an HTML document.
- **`<html>`**: The root element for the webpage.
- **`<head>`**: Contains meta-information like the title.
- **`<title>`**: Sets the webpage title in the browser tab.
- **`<body>`**: Contains everything you see on the webpage.
- **`<h1>`, `<p>`, `<a>`**: Tags to add headings, paragraphs, and links.

Creating Your First Webpage

1. Open any **text editor** (like VS Code or Notepad++).
2. Save a new file as `index.html`.
3. Copy and paste the example HTML code above.
4. Open the file in your browser to see your first webpage!

CSS: Adding Style to Your Webpage

CSS stands for **Cascading Style Sheets**. It's used to style and design webpages, such as changing colors, fonts, and layout.

How to Add CSS

There are three main ways to add CSS to a webpage:

1. **Inline CSS**: Style applied directly inside an HTML tag.
2. **Internal CSS**: Style written in the `<head>` section using the `<style>` tag.
3. **External CSS**: Style written in a separate `.css` file.

Example: Adding Inline and Internal CSS

html

```html
<!DOCTYPE html>
<html>
  <head>
    <title>Styled Webpage</title>
    <style>
      body {
        background-color: lightblue;
        font-family: Arial, sans-serif;
      }
      h1 {
        color: navy;
        text-align: center;
      }
      p {
        color: darkred;
        font-size: 18px;
      }
    </style>
  </head>
  <body>
    <h1>Welcome to My Styled Webpage</h1>
    <p>This is a paragraph with custom styles.</p>
  </body>
</html>
```

What It Does:

- Changes the background color of the page.
- Makes the heading navy blue and centered.
- Styles the paragraph with dark red text and a larger font.

Python and the Web

Python can be used to build websites using **web frameworks** like **Flask** or **Django**. These tools allow you to combine HTML and CSS with Python code to create dynamic websites.

For now, here's a quick example using Flask to serve an HTML page:

Setting Up Flask (Optional)

1. Install Flask: Run `pip install flask` in your terminal.
2. Create a file called `app.py` and add this code:

```python
from flask import Flask

app = Flask(__name__)

@app.route("/")
def home():
    return "<h1>Welcome to My Python-Powered Webpage!</h1>"

if __name__ == "__main__":
    app.run(debug=True)
```

3. Run the script: `python app.py`.
4. Open your browser and visit `http://127.0.0.1:5000`.

Project: Building a Simple Personal Webpage

Let's create a webpage with HTML and CSS that introduces yourself.

Step 1: Create the HTML File

Save this code in a file called index.html:

html

```
<!DOCTYPE html>
<html>
  <head>
    <title>About Me</title>
    <style>
      body {
        font-family: Arial, sans-serif;
        background-color: #f4f4f4;
        margin: 0;
        padding: 0;
      }
      h1 {
        color: #333;
        text-align: center;
        margin-top: 20px;
      }
      p {
        text-align: center;
        font-size: 18px;
        color: #666;
      }
    </style>
  </head>
  <body>
    <h1>Hi, I'm [Your Name]</h1>
    <p>Welcome to my first webpage! I'm learning to code,
and this is my personal site.</p>
  </body>
</html>
```

Step 2: View the Webpage

1. Open the file in your browser.
2. You'll see a simple, styled webpage introducing yourself.

Practice Exercises

1. **Basic Webpage**: Create an HTML page with:
   - A heading (`<h1>`) introducing your favorite hobby.
   - A paragraph (`<p>`) explaining why you love it.
   - A link (`<a>`) to a website about that hobby.
2. **Add CSS**: Style the page using CSS. Change the background color, font size, and text alignment.
3. **Flask Challenge (Optional)**: Create a basic Flask app that displays a webpage with the message "Hello, World!" when you visit the homepage.

Reflection: What Did You Learn?

1. How do HTML and CSS work together to create webpages?
2. What is the purpose of tags like `<h1>`, `<p>`, and `<a>` in HTML?
3. How can programming languages like Python interact with web development?

What's Next?

Congratulations! You've learned the basics of programming, built projects, and even explored web development. In the final chapter, we'll discuss **next steps for your coding journey**, including how to continue learning, showcase your projects, and explore advanced topics.

The world of coding is wide open—let's get ready for what's next!

Chapter 13: Small Coding Projects to Build Your Confidence

The best way to learn programming is to build things—no matter how simple they are! Practice solidifies what you've learned, strengthens your problem-solving skills, and boosts your confidence as a coder.

In this chapter, you'll work on **beginner-friendly projects** that reinforce key programming concepts like loops, conditions, functions, and user input. By the end, you'll have a portfolio of small programs that show off your skills.

The projects include:

1. **A Number Guessing Game**
2. **A Basic Calculator**
3. **A To-Do List Program**
4. **A Simple Password Validator**

Each project comes with explanations and step-by-step code to help you succeed.

Project 1: Number Guessing Game

Test your coding skills by building a fun guessing game where the user tries to guess a secret number.

What You'll Practice

- Loops (`while`)
- Conditions (`if-else`)
- User input

Code

python

```python
import random

def guessing_game():
    print("Welcome to the Number Guessing Game!")
    print("I'm thinking of a number between 1 and 10.")

    secret_number = random.randint(1, 10)   # Generate a
random number
    attempts = 0

    while True:
        guess = input("Enter your guess: ")

        if not guess.isdigit():   # Check for valid input
            print("Please enter a number.")
            continue

        guess = int(guess)
        attempts += 1

        if guess == secret_number:
            print(f"Congratulations! You guessed it in
{attempts} tries.")
            break
        elif guess < secret_number:
            print("Too low! Try again.")
```

```python
        else:
            print("Too high! Try again.")

guessing_game()
```

Project 2: Basic Calculator

Build a simple calculator that performs addition, subtraction, multiplication, and division.

What You'll Practice

- User input
- Functions
- Conditions (if-else)

Code

python

```python
def calculator():
    print("Simple Calculator")
    print("Choose an operation: add, subtract, multiply, divide")

    while True:
        operation = input("Enter operation (or 'exit' to quit): ").lower()

        if operation == "exit":
            print("Goodbye!")
            break

        if operation not in ["add", "subtract", "multiply", "divide"]:
            print("Invalid operation. Try again.")
            continue

        try:
            num1 = float(input("Enter the first number: "))
            num2 = float(input("Enter the second number: "))
        except ValueError:
            print("Please enter valid numbers.")
            continue
```

```python
    if operation == "add":
        print(f"Result: {num1 + num2}")
    elif operation == "subtract":
        print(f"Result: {num1 - num2}")
    elif operation == "multiply":
        print(f"Result: {num1 * num2}")
    elif operation == "divide":
        if num2 == 0:
            print("Cannot divide by zero.")
        else:
            print(f"Result: {num1 / num2}")

calculator()
```

Project 3: Simple To-Do List Program

Create a program that lets the user add, view, and remove tasks from a to-do list.

What You'll Practice

- Lists
- Loops (while)
- Conditions

Code

```python
python

def to_do_list():
    tasks = []

    print("Welcome to the To-Do List Program!")
    print("Options: add, view, remove, exit")

    while True:
        action = input("What would you like to do?
").lower()

        if action == "add":
            task = input("Enter a task: ")
            tasks.append(task)
            print(f"Task '{task}' added!")

        elif action == "view":
            print("\nYour To-Do List:")
            if not tasks:
                print("No tasks yet!")
            else:
                for index, task in enumerate(tasks,
start=1):
                    print(f"{index}. {task}")
            print()

        elif action == "remove":
```

```python
            print("Your To-Do List:")
            for index, task in enumerate(tasks, start=1):
                print(f"{index}. {task}")
            try:
                task_number = int(input("Enter the task
number to remove: "))
                removed_task = tasks.pop(task_number - 1)
                print(f"Removed '{removed_task}'.")
            except (ValueError, IndexError):
                print("Invalid task number. Please try
again.")

        elif action == "exit":
            print("Goodbye! Keep being productive!")
            break

        else:
            print("Invalid option. Try again.")

to_do_list()
```

Project 4: Password Validator

Build a program that checks if a password meets basic security requirements.

What You'll Practice

- Conditions (if-else)
- Loops and input validation

Code

python

```python
def password_validator():
    print("Password Validator: Your password must meet
these rules:")
    print("- At least 8 characters long")
    print("- Includes both letters and numbers")
    print("- Contains at least one uppercase letter")

    while True:
        password = input("Enter a password: ")

        if len(password) < 8:
            print("Password is too short. Try again.")
        elif not any(char.isdigit() for char in password):
            print("Password must include at least one
number. Try again.")
        elif not any(char.isupper() for char in password):
            print("Password must include at least one
uppercase letter. Try again.")
        else:
            print("Password is valid! Well done.")
            break

password_validator()
```

Tips for Building Projects

1. **Start Small**: Focus on one feature at a time. Test and debug as you go.
2. **Think Through the Logic**: Before writing code, plan how the program will work (inputs, outputs, and steps).
3. **Add Personal Touches**: Customize the projects—add extra features or improve the user interface.
4. **Fix Errors**: Don't get discouraged when you encounter bugs! Debugging is part of coding.

Reflection: What Did You Learn?

1. How did building these projects help you practice key coding skills?
2. Which project was the most fun or challenging for you?
3. What other programs would you like to create using what you've learned?

What's Next?

Congratulations! 🎉 You've completed your journey through this book and built a solid foundation in coding. In the next (and final) section, we'll discuss where to go from here—how to continue learning, share your projects, and explore exciting paths as a programmer.

Remember: Every project you build brings you one step closer to mastering programming. Keep coding and creating—your future is bright!

Chapter 14: Next Steps: Exploring Coding Languages and Tools

You've made it! By completing this book, you've built a strong foundation in coding, learned essential concepts, and created real programs. Now it's time to explore where coding can take you.

In this chapter, you'll learn:

1. **Popular coding languages** to expand your skills beyond Python.
2. Key tools and frameworks for specific fields, like **web development**, **game development**, and **data science**.
3. Guidance on choosing your next steps based on your interests and career goals.

By the end of this chapter, you'll be ready to continue your coding journey with excitement and a clear sense of direction.

Exploring Other Coding Languages

While Python is an excellent beginner language, there are many other languages that power the tech world. Each has its own strengths and common uses:

Language	What It's Used For	Why Learn It?
JavaScript	Web development (frontend and backend)	Adds interactivity to websites.
HTML & CSS	Web page structure and design	Essential for building websites.
Java	Mobile apps, enterprise software	Powers Android apps and large systems.
C++	Game development, high-performance apps	Used for complex, fast applications.
C#	Game development with Unity	Great for building video games.
SQL	Databases and data management	Retrieve and analyze large datasets.
R	Data science and statistics	Analyze data and create visualizations.

Fields to Explore with Coding

1. Web Development

Web developers create websites and web applications.

- **Frontend Development**: Focuses on what users see and interact with. Learn **HTML**, **CSS**, and **JavaScript**.
- **Backend Development**: Manages the server and database. Use Python with **Flask** or **Django** frameworks.
- **Full-Stack Development**: Combines both frontend and backend skills.

Next Tools to Learn:

- **Frameworks**: Flask, Django (Python), React, Vue.js, Node.js
- **Tools**: Git, GitHub, VS Code

2. Game Development

If you enjoy games, you can build your own using coding skills!

- Use **Python** with libraries like **Pygame** to create 2D games.
- Learn **C#** with **Unity** for advanced 2D and 3D games.
- Explore **C++** for high-performance games with engines like **Unreal Engine**.

Next Tools to Learn:

- **Engines**: Unity, Unreal Engine
- **Libraries**: Pygame, Godot

3. Data Science and Machine Learning

Data scientists analyze data to find patterns and make predictions.

- Python is widely used in data science with libraries like **Pandas**, **NumPy**, and **Matplotlib**.
- Learn **SQL** to work with databases.
- Explore **machine learning** using tools like **Scikit-learn** and **TensorFlow**.

Next Tools to Learn:

- **Libraries**: Pandas, NumPy, Matplotlib, TensorFlow, Scikit-learn
- **Tools**: Jupyter Notebook, Google Colab

---

4. Mobile App Development

Create apps for phones and tablets.

- Use **Python** with frameworks like **Kivy** or **BeeWare** for simple apps.
- Learn **Java** or **Kotlin** for Android development.
- Use **Swift** for iOS development.

Next Tools to Learn:

- **Frameworks**: Kivy, React Native, Flutter
- **Languages**: Java, Swift, Kotlin

5. Cybersecurity

Cybersecurity focuses on protecting systems and data from hackers.

- Learn Python for automating security tools and penetration testing.
- Explore tools like **Wireshark** and **Kali Linux** for ethical hacking.

Next Tools to Learn:

- **Skills**: Networking basics, encryption, ethical hacking
- **Languages**: Python, Bash scripting

Choosing Your Path

How do you decide what to explore next? Here are some questions to guide you:

1. **What excites you?** Do you want to build websites, create games, analyze data, or develop apps?
2. **What are your goals?** Are you coding for fun, a career change, or to start a business?
3. **What industries interest you?** Technology, finance, health, gaming, or something else?

Building Your Portfolio

A great way to showcase your coding skills is to create a portfolio of projects. You can:

- Add your code to **GitHub**—a platform to store and share projects.
- Build a personal website to display your work.
- Start a blog or YouTube channel to document your learning journey.

Project Ideas for Your Portfolio:

1. A personal website showcasing your skills.
2. A game built with Pygame or Unity.
3. A web app using Flask or Django.
4. A data analysis project using Python libraries.

Keep Learning

The world of programming is always evolving, so it's important to keep learning. Here's how:

1. **Take Online Courses**: Platforms like **Coursera**, **Udemy**, and **freeCodeCamp** offer beginner-friendly courses.
2. **Join Coding Communities**: Participate in forums like **Stack Overflow** or join coding groups on **Discord** and **Reddit**.
3. **Build Projects**: The more you practice, the better you'll get.
4. **Learn from Others**: Explore open-source projects on GitHub to see how other programmers write code.

Reflection: What's Next for You?

Take a moment to think about your next steps:

1. Which coding field excites you the most?
2. What new tools or languages will you explore first?
3. What project can you start building right now?

A Final Word

Congratulations on completing this book! You've taken your first steps into the exciting world of programming. Whether you choose to build websites, games, apps, or analyze data, remember that coding is a skill you can always improve with practice and curiosity.

The possibilities are endless—keep exploring, building, and learning. The coding world is yours to create!

Chapter 15: Becoming a Lifelong Coder: Resources and Communities

Congratulations—you've taken your first steps into the world of coding! But coding is a lifelong journey, and the more you practice, the better you'll become. The key to growing as a programmer is to keep learning, exploring, and connecting with others who share your passion.

In this chapter, you'll discover:

1. **Online resources** to continue learning (free and paid).
2. The value of **coding communities** and where to find them.
3. How to grow through **challenges** and real-world projects.
4. How to stay motivated and inspired on your programming journey.

By the end, you'll have all the tools you need to keep coding, learning, and improving for years to come.

1. Online Resources for Learning

The internet is full of amazing resources that help you level up your coding skills. Here are some of the best platforms for beginners and beyond:

Free Learning Platforms

- **freeCodeCamp**: A free, interactive platform to learn web development, Python, data analysis, and more.
- **The Odin Project**: A full, free curriculum for learning web development, covering HTML, CSS, JavaScript, and beyond.
- **CS50 by Harvard**: A free introduction to computer science for absolute beginners.

Paid Platforms with Beginner-Friendly Courses

- **Codecademy**: Interactive lessons on Python, JavaScript, web development, and more.
- **Udemy**: Affordable courses with lifetime access—search for beginner-friendly courses in your chosen language.
- **Coursera**: University-level courses that often include free options, like Python for Everyone.

Video Learning

- **YouTube**: Channels like "Programming with Mosh," "freeCodeCamp.org," and "Traversy Media" offer free tutorials.
- **edX**: Video courses from top universities on coding fundamentals.

2. Coding Communities: Learn and Grow Together

Learning to code is easier when you're part of a supportive community. Coding communities allow you to ask questions, learn from others, share your work, and stay motivated.

Where to Find Coding Communities

- **Stack Overflow**: The go-to forum for asking and answering coding questions.
- **Reddit**: Subreddits like **r/learnprogramming, r/Python**, and **r/webdev** are great for beginners.
- **Discord and Slack Groups**: Platforms like **freeCodeCamp's Discord server** or coding-focused Slack groups allow you to chat with other learners in real time.
- **GitHub**: A platform to host, share, and collaborate on projects. Explore open-source projects and contribute when ready.
- **Twitter and LinkedIn**: Follow programmers and join discussions about coding trends.

3. Participate in Coding Challenges

Challenges are a fun way to apply what you've learned, test your skills, and build confidence. They also help you practice problem-solving—a key skill for any programmer.

Best Platforms for Coding Challenges

- **HackerRank**: Beginner-friendly challenges in Python, JavaScript, and other languages.
- **LeetCode**: Great for building problem-solving skills and preparing for coding interviews.
- **Codewars**: Practice coding with fun, gamified challenges.
- **Advent of Code**: A yearly event with coding puzzles released every December.

4. Building Real-World Projects

The best way to learn coding is by **building projects**. Projects allow you to combine skills, learn by doing, and showcase your abilities to others.

Project Ideas to Keep Learning

1. **Personal Website**: Create a website with HTML, CSS, and Python.
2. **Budget Tracker**: Build a program that tracks income and expenses.
3. **Weather App**: Use APIs to display real-time weather data for any city.
4. **Simple Game**: Use Python and Pygame to create a small game like "Guess the Number" or "Snake."
5. **Data Visualizer**: Analyze and visualize data with Python libraries like Matplotlib.

Tip: Share your projects on GitHub or build a portfolio website to track your progress.

5. Staying Motivated on Your Coding Journey

Coding is challenging, and it's normal to feel stuck or frustrated at times. Here's how to stay motivated:

- **Celebrate small wins**: Every program you write, no matter how small, is progress.
- **Learn at your pace**: Don't compare your journey to others—focus on your own growth.
- **Find inspiration**: Follow stories of self-taught programmers and explore tech blogs.
- **Join a support group**: Connect with friends, mentors, or online learners who can encourage you when things get tough.

---

6. Where to Go Next: Specialize and Explore

Now that you know the basics, you can explore specific fields and choose a path that excites you:

- **Web Development**: Learn HTML, CSS, JavaScript, Flask, and Django.
- **Game Development**: Explore Pygame, Unity (C#), or Unreal Engine (C++).
- **Data Science**: Learn Pandas, NumPy, Matplotlib, and machine learning tools.
- **Mobile App Development**: Use Kivy, Flutter, or Java/Kotlin for Android apps.
- **Cybersecurity**: Dive into Python scripting, networking, and ethical hacking.

Remember: The coding world is vast, and there's always something new to learn. Choose an area you love and go deep!

Key Takeaways

1. There are **endless resources**—online courses, coding challenges, and video tutorials—to help you keep learning.
2. Join **communities** like Stack Overflow, Reddit, and GitHub to connect with other coders.
3. **Practice regularly** with coding challenges and build real-world projects to sharpen your skills.
4. Stay curious and patient—becoming a great coder takes time, practice, and a love for learning.

Final Words: Your Coding Journey Has Just Begun

Learning to code is not a destination—it's a journey. By completing this book, you've gained the skills and mindset to tackle real-world coding challenges. Whether you're building apps, games, websites, or analyzing data, you now have the foundation to keep growing.

Keep exploring, keep building, and keep coding. The possibilities are endless, and your journey has only just begun.

Happy coding—and welcome to the amazing world of programming!

Conclusion: Your Journey to Coding Success

Congratulations on reaching the end of this book! Whether you started with no coding experience or had a small head start, you've made incredible progress. You've learned how to write code, solve problems, build projects, and think like a programmer. That's no small achievement!

By completing this journey, you've gained more than just the ability to write programs—you've unlocked a skill that opens doors to **creativity**, **career opportunities**, and **problem-solving** in today's digital world.

What You've Accomplished

Let's celebrate your success and reflect on how far you've come:

1. **You've built a foundation**: From understanding variables and loops to mastering functions and basic Object-Oriented Programming.
2. **You've written your own programs**: Whether it was a calculator, to-do list, or a guessing game, you've brought ideas to life through code.
3. **You've gained confidence**: Debugging errors, solving challenges, and completing projects have shown you that coding isn't magic—it's a skill anyone can learn with practice.

Why Coding Matters

Learning to code doesn't just teach you how to program—it changes the way you think. Coding trains your mind to:

- **Break big problems into smaller steps**.
- **Think logically and creatively** to find solutions.
- **Persevere and adapt** when you hit obstacles—because every coder knows that bugs are just learning opportunities!

These skills go beyond programming and are useful in any career or life challenge.

What Comes Next?

Your coding journey doesn't stop here—it's only just beginning. Here are a few steps you can take to keep moving forward:

1. **Build More Projects**: Start small, but challenge yourself to create apps, websites, or games that excite you. Share your work with others!
2. **Explore New Tools and Languages**: Learn JavaScript for web development, SQL for databases, or Python libraries for data science.
3. **Join the Coding Community**: Stay connected with other learners and developers through forums, coding challenges, and open-source projects.
4. **Keep Learning**: Coding is always evolving, and there's always more to explore. Take online courses, read tutorials, or follow tech trends to stay inspired.

Final Encouragement

If there's one thing to take away from this book, it's this: **you can code**. No matter where you're starting from, coding is a skill that anyone can learn with practice, patience, and curiosity.

Every program you write, every bug you fix, and every project you complete brings you one step closer to becoming the coder you want to be.

So keep going. Keep practicing. Keep building.

The digital world is full of possibilities—and now you have the skills to create them.

Thank you for taking this journey. Now go out there, write some code, and make something amazing!

Happy coding!
— A.J. Smales